ALCATRAZ

TED NEEDHAM-HOWARD NEEDHAM

ALCATRAZ

TED NEEDHAM-HOWARD NEEDHAM

CELESTIAL ARTS
Millbrae, California

Copyright © 1976 by Ted Needham and Howard Needham

CELESTIAL ARTS
231 Adrian Road
Millbrae, California 94030

First Printing, May 1976
Made in the United States of America

Library of Congress Cataloging in Publication Data

Needham, Ted.
    Alcatraz.

    1. United States. Penitentiary, Alcatraz Island,
Calif. I. Needham, Howard. II. Title.
HV9474.A4N43   365'.9794'61   76-11350
ISBN 0-89087-129-9

    2 3 4 5 6 7 — 81 80 79 77

PREFACE

When my brother and I were boys in San Francisco, *The Rock* was just an island in the bay with an old Army barracks where supposedly hard-line military prisoners were confined.

Later when we were journalists on competing dailies, *The Rock* was a federal penitentiary where the nation's worst mobsters and criminals served their time. A community of criminals who had lost their rights as people.

We didn't think about it much. It didn't weigh on our minds, except on those few occasions when *The Rock's* restless inmates rocketed the little island into national headlines. Then we thought of *The Rock* as "that place no newsman can crack."

Now we wonder at our youthful ability to be so unconcerned about a community of fellow human beings. Today the nation's whole penal system is under scrutiny. Changes are being made. More are in the planning stage.

We were very aware of this new scrutiny as we clambered over empty, vacant Alcatraz in September 1973.

We wanted to photograph "the end of an agony" as we thought of it. Not to give any ongoing currency to the agony, but in some measure to mark its end.

The men who administered Alcatraz, the inmates who peopled it, the guards and their families, are long gone from *The Rock.* There are no traces anywhere of any single individual's tenure there, only the decaying plant that once housed America's most hardened criminal community. That is the feeling of the place. The empty corridors, cells, towers and workshops seem to speak for all who lived there—the jailers and the jailed.

Ted thought it fitting to photograph *The Rock* empty, the way we found it, without human company, swept by fog and wind, bound by chill tides and just there— waiting.

Howard Needham
Kentfield, California

ACKNOWLEDGMENTS

We are grateful to the U.S. Bureau of Prisons and the Golden Gate National Recreation Area of the National Park Service for their assistance in gathering much of the material presented here.

Very special thanks go to Superintendent William J. Whalen of the Golden Gate National Recreation Area, to J. Jerry Rumburg, Supervisory Park Ranger, Alcatraz, and to David B. Ames, Chief of Interpretation for the recreation area. They gave generously of their time, facilities and knowledge of *The Rock*. Without their help it is doubtful that these particular photographs could have been recorded in September 1973. The island became a national park in October and its silent, vacant days were gone.

Finally, we are grateful to Misa who correlated notes, negatives, drafts and text, and who maintained a certain productive order of time, men and materials throughout the effort.

Alcatraz has been many things in its time but with the single exception of its lighthouse it has never served man well. Don Juan Manuel de Ayala found it populated by pelicans in 1775 and named it *Isla de Los Alcatraces*—"Island of the Pelicans." In 1846 the slightly corrupt and last Mexican governor of California tried to settle a purely personal debt by granting title to the island to one Julian Workman, an American then living in the city of St. Francis. This relatively modest misuse of *The Rock* failed when the "Bear Flag Revolt" intervened, leaving all California land grants under title-cloud. After years of litigation the island became a possession of the federal government of the United States.

Insofar as history records the Spanish colonial governors appear to have sensed the negative character of the place. They are totally innocent of any attempt to make use of it, or to build on it. Alcatraz was a nude twelve-acre rock when American construction crews debarked there in 1853 to build the nation's first fortification on its newly acquired Pacific Coast.

Fort Alcatraz was christened officially five years later. It consisted of three batteries of artillery, 43 guns with supporting barracks, water cisterns, powder magazines and shellproof dugouts. One hundred and thirty soldiers manned the fort. The lighthouse was completed in 1859 and has been serving man as a mariner's beacon ever since.

Even during this first effort to shape Alcatraz to some useful purpose the island manifested its inhospitality. There was no water. Water for the workmen and the mortar mixing box had to be barged out from the city. The very substance of the island defied man's use. *The Rock's* shale composition was useless as a construction material. Fired bricks were ferried from the city's brickyards and granite ballast blocks from the harbor's graveyard of clipper ships were used to reinforce the bricks.

The Rock when completed in 1858 was a formidable fortress by 19th century standards. But with destiny's help Alcatraz retained its obduracy. The fort never fired a shot in anger because no enemy ever roused its garrison. It was a fort that never had occasion to exercise its purpose.

Gradually the Army commenced to use its storerooms and other adaptive quarters as prison cells for military offenders, drunks, deserters and minor recalcitrants. By 1868, only ten short years after its christening, Fort Alcatraz officially was a military prison, though the artillery garrison remained on the island.

The island served as a fortress-prison from 1868 until 1933 when the War Department determined it was no longer needed for military purposes. During that 65 years, varied categories of unfortunate humans caught in the web of military and national security regulations, the Civil War, the so-called Indian Wars, Spanish-American War, the war with Mexico, World Wars I and II, and other less notable events passed through *The Rock's* brick-and-iron facilities.

By some quirk of military logic *The Rock* in 1900 became for a very brief period a health spa. Soldiers returning home from the Cuban and Philippine campaigns with tropical ailments were sent there to convalesce. *The Rock* turned them back. Its fog-ridden winds and chill atmosphere produced irrefutable evidence among the victimized patients that Alcatraz was no place for sick men. The Army sent them to milder climes.

Only once in its history did *The Rock* allure man. That was on April 18, 1906, when San Franciscans were awakened by what has been termed "The Great Earthquake." For a few days, as the residents fled from fire, a few falling buildings and the Army's dynamiting of many unsafe structures, *The Rock* looked pretty good to some who saw it as a possible island of safety.

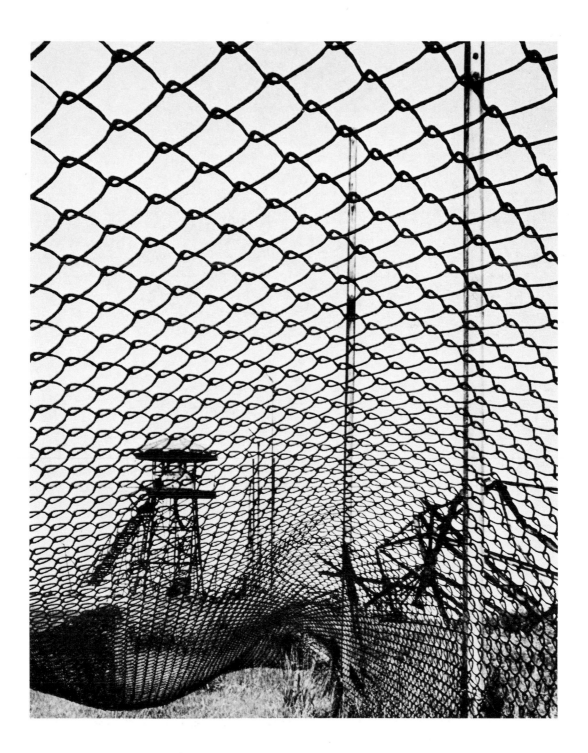

And it did serve during "The Great Fire" which followed the earthquake as an island of safety—to 150 civilian prisoners who had survived the collapse of the city's jail and Hall of Justice. Herded for 52 hours about the stricken city by militiamen in search of a safe and secure sanctuary, these unfortunates were finally taken by their keepers to *The Rock* where they shared food and lodging with their military counterparts for ten days.

This curious spark of hospitality presaged the end of Alcatraz as a fortress. Eleven months later the island was designated the Pacific Branch of the U.S. Military Prison and ceased to be a fort altogether, largely due to advances in the development of U.S. Naval artillery which outmoded *The Rock's* fixed batteries.

Outwardly Alcatraz changed hardly at all. Construction of the main prison building, which today still houses the main cell blocks, continued and was completed in 1909. The artillerymen and their guns left the island. The guards and their prisoners remained. In 1915 Alcatraz was renamed a "disciplinary barracks." It remained an Army prison until that chilly midnight of December 31, 1933, when it became officially a federal penitentiary.

The Rock's most notorious phase commenced that night and, like its previous phases, this one too would become unnecessary and a negative asset within three decades.

There is a certain mythology about *The Rock* today, a mythology springing from its history and the character of its first civilian warden, James A. Johnston.

Like most myths it becomes less and less true as time passes. Thus *The Rock*, as criminals referred to it in dread tones in the '30s, became a different institution in the '40s and changed again in the '50s. By the time the late Attorney General Robert F. Kennedy announced its closing in June of 1962, three wardens later, it was very different from the institution established by Warden Johnston.

Old time prison officials and penologists raised their eyebrows in 1934 when it became known that Attorney General Homer Cummings had asked Johnston to plan, supervise construction and become warden of the nation's toughest penitentiary. For Johnston was not famous for his toughness, rather he was known for his successes as a young reform warden at Folsom and San Quentin.

Long retired from his first career as a penologist, Johnston was a senior banking official when he got the call in 1933 from the attorney general, asking him to return to penology, to create and administer an escape-proof penal institution which would incarcerate the nation's most unregenerate criminals.

At Folsom prison in 1913, and later at San Quentin, the young Johnston stood for a rehabilitative emphasis in American penology rather than a punitive one. At Alcatraz Johnston revealed another side of his remarkable character. With a congressional appropriation of $260,000 and the island's original prison building still intact, he proceeded to create *The Rock* as it was feared by outlaws of the Prohibition and post-Prohibition eras.

He arrived on the island January 2, 1934, and for weeks the soft-spoken bespectacled, white-thatched, slender and still hale old man prowled every nook and cranny of the place. In his mind's eye he envisaged a prison area encompassing the main cell blocks, workhouses, offices, storerooms and recreation yard, entirely encased in wire mesh and barbed wire, manned by guards on mesh-protected catwalks inside and outside the buildings. The angle of vision from every point of guard-surveillance, including those of the outside towers, was plotted in Johnston's mind and reduced to blueprint specifications.

Inside the old prison building rose tier-blocks of one-man cells, each cell eight feet long by five feet wide, each with its own toilet, wash basin and wall-bunk. Wire-mesh-protected catwalks for the guards ringed the tier blocks, commanding a view of every prisoner-corridor and every cell door. Electrically controlled block-locks, capable of remote operation if necessary, opened and closed the cell doors, corridor by corridor. Surveillance of every inmate was continuous throughout 24 hours, at work, asleep, in the recreation yard and during the brief walks from cell block to work site.

When the men of Alcatraz went to eat they merely passed through an open pair of iron gates whose bars were the only dividing line between the tier blocks, the mess hall and the kitchen. All three facilities were under the same roof and on the same floor. Between meals the gates were kept locked but the sounds of cooking and the smells of food wafted up to the highest and most remote cell in the top tier, announcing the menu beforehand.

Down on the ground floor, "Broadway," the central prisoner's corridor, always waxed to a mirror-like sheen, led directly into the large immaculate mess hall. The convicts ate ringed by guards and under a ceiling studded with tear gas outlets, ready for automatic use should the occasion arise.

Visitors to the island passed through metal detecting devices, as did guards and prisoners, at the landing dock, at all entrances and exits of the main cell house, and at places of ingress and egress to and from the workshops. The main entrance to the prison was through a series of three rooms, each one a bastion of observation and security.

The outer room or armory had two guards, one to peer at the visitor through a bullet-proof panel and, if satisfied that the visitor was "safe," electrically manipulate a steel plate back from the lock, into which a second guard manually inserted a key and opened the door. The ensuing two doors were of solid plate steel and steel bars.

This three-stage entrance worked as well against would-be escapers as it would against any invaders. The single guard in the forward part of the armory was so encased behind locks, steel and bullet-proof glass that he would remain secure from any attack from within or without the main building.

Outside, in the five guard towers and on the catwalks, guards armed with .30 caliber carbines and high-powered rifles (two guns per man), maintained a vise-like vigil over the island dock, the work areas, the recreation yard, the rooftops, the roadways on which the convicts marched to and from workshops. The combined perspective from five towers blanketed the island's land surface and commanded bay waters to virtually all points of the compass.

The Rock was a twelve-acre cage, separated from its world-famous, gay and glamorous metropolis by one and one-fourth miles of vicious cold tides which swirled and gurgled by at six, seven, eight and sometimes nine knots.

That was its physical make-up. Psychologically it was just as confining. If anything inherently negative can have an outward thrust, a positive crushing strength, the original prison program laid down by Warden Johnston had it. Confinement on *The Rock* was not society's ultimate punishment. That remained death by execution. But *The Rock* during its first four years certainly was America's penultimate sentence for criminals.

In accordance with the attorney general's instructions, Johnston's program made no pretense at rehabilitation. It was a complete reversal of his San Quentin philosophy. Alcatraz was to be a prison of "maximum security and minimum privilege."

When that first contingent of 53 felons, manacled, shuffled out of their blacked-out Pullman car onto *The Rock's* landing dock, they must have blanched at the wire-festooned cliffs, walls, towers, catwalks and huge main cell house towering over them.

They arrived the morning of August 15, 1934, after traveling from Atlanta in the sealed train, manacled, sleepless, without air conditioning, allowed to move from their seats only to the lavatory under guard. They were sweaty and they stank, partly from the heat and partly from nervousness.

Their legs and ankles were swollen and the

manacles hurt. One man sobbed aloud and tears rolled down his face as he stood on the dock gazing up. He and his fellow inmates had been transported still inside their sealed car by ferry-barge from Belvedere Island, directly into *The Rock's* ferry slip. The instant close-up of *The Rock* from its own base had a shattering impact.

The scene was repeated several times, at weekly intervals, until *The Rock's* inmate population stood at 242. Every man of the 242 went through the same mind-crushing introduction to his new place of confinement.

It was a select collection of the nation's worst criminals. These men already had *proved* that they were tough, obdurate, violent, calculating and, in many cases, psychoneurotic. In their previous prisons they had constituted an intolerable harassment of ordinary prison routine, making any attempts to rehabilitate other prisoners impossible. They were rejects from society's rejected. Alcatraz was their last stopping place. All were lifers or long termers. Many had shown that they could kill while trying to escape.

Among them were the famed gangsters, killers and gunmen of the early '20s, men who had cut a swath of criminal violence across the nation before being brought to book by state and federal enforcement agencies, men like Al "Scarface" Capone, Machine Gun Kelly, Birdman Robert Stroud, mail train robber Roy Gardner, kidnapper Arthur "Doc" Barker and his tough gunmate Al Karpis. Of these only Barker gave serious trouble. He was shot down on a rocky Alcatraz shore

as he attempted to swim from the island.

The other former underworld bosses in one way or another served their time without dramatic incident. Capone asked for and was granted an isolation cell. He worked in the laundry until, incurably ill, he was paroled to spend a few short years with his family before dying in Miami. Birdman Stroud did not practice his birdlore on Alcatraz as is popularly believed. He had already done that in other federal prisons before coming to *The Rock* with a record of chronic prison violence. At Alcatraz he served his time in isolation, a condition imposed in the presidential commutation of his death sentence to life imprisonment. Mail robber Gardner was a charter inmate in 1934, became a model prisoner and was paroled in 1938, only to commit suicide in a hotel room a year later. Machine Gun Kelly, a "big man" in the underworld, lost that image as he studiously evaded the inevitable yard confrontations by fellow inmates. He became a quiet loner.

The threat to Warden Johnston's new concept of escape-proof incarceration was not to come from the underworld's famed bosses. The real menace would emerge from the ranks of *The Rock's* lesser known inmates.

But before these few daring men would make their desperate bids they would have to study for months-on-end an intricate physical and administrative security system which, from their first day on the island, convinced most inmates that escape from Alcatraz was truly impossible.

Warden Johnston began by severing their connections with the outside world and denying them the relief of conversation. Each inmate was permitted only one visitor a month and that visitor had to be blood-related or spouse. The men lived under the "Rule of Silence" which was later dropped. They could not speak in the cell house or the mess hall. Infringement of the "Rule of Silence" in those days meant "the hole" in D block.

The prisoner saw no newspapers, heard no radios. Even his once-a-month visitor was instructed not to discuss public events with him, only family matters. The prisoner could not discuss *The Rock*, only his personal problems. Inmate and visitor sat on opposite sides of a two-foot-thick wall and looked at each other through a clear panel set in inches-thick, bullet-proof glass which, incidentally, was soundproof. The conversation was by telephone, and if either the visitor or the inmate broke the rules of conversation, a monitoring guard would break the telephone circuit.

Through the little clear panel the visitor's view of his relative's face was against a background of tiers of cells rising from the floor sheen of "Broadway." The inmate set in the open end-corridor of the cell house, his back to corridor traffic and the sounds of inmates in their cells. There were four "visiting" stools on the inmates' side.

All mail, in or out of *The Rock*, was censored.

Even "inanimate" things from the outside world such as brand-name soap, candy, soft drinks, magazines and other canteen-type items were forbidden. Alcatraz had no PX or canteen store. Money was forbidden in the hands of prisoners. There were no trustees. All items of a game nature and any object that could be construed as a potential device for gambling was contraband, and the sentence for possession meant time in one of the "hole" cells and loss of good-time credits.

The inmate's day was incredibly lonely. He spent fourteen hours a day in his locked cell, in silence, every day of the year. He was awakened at 6:30 A.M. and given time to wash and dress. A few moments later the electric locks or a guard opened his cell door. He then stepped out into the "Prisoner's Corridor" which passed in front of his cell and took his place in line to march to the mess hall where he ate breakfast, in total silence. After breakfast he returned in silence to his cell for the prisoner count. This completed throughout the cell house, his door was reopened and he was escorted under guard to his workshop or maintenance assignment, and there counted again.

Lunch was at 11:30 A.M. and followed another silent return to his cell, lockup and count. When the door opened again after a quick wash he marched in line to the voiceless mess hall. Lunch's conclusion meant a return to his cell which was locked again and reopened after a brief rest period. He then marched back to work at 1:00 P.M.

This procedure was repeated at work-day's end, again when he marched to dinner, and upon his return from dinner. Final lockup came immediately following dinner, at 5:30 P.M., with every man in his cell, alone and silent. Cell lights went off at 9:30.

Only inmates in good standing were permitted to use the recreation yard in those early years, and these only on Sundays and holidays. The sound of shuffling feet, the clanging of iron doors, the counting and the endless marching in single file, and the smell of cooking from the mess hall were the only punctuations of the monotonous days. The counting of men was incessant, every half-hour, and was *The Rock's* key technique in detecting any escape attempt.

Alcatraz offered no encouragement to good behavior in the early '30s, only punishment for infraction of the rules. Such punishment could mean days in the utterly soundless pitch blackness of a solitary "hole" cell on a diet of bread and water -- and the loss of good-time credits, the inmate's earned currency toward parole or transfer to a conventional prison.

This relentless combination of impenetrable physical plant and almost unendurable discipline was Warden Johnston's own creation. It surprised those old prison hands who recalled his earlier rehabilitative administrations at Folsom and San Quentin.

But if Warden Johnston had escalated physical containment and prison discipline to a new peak in American penology, he had done it well. Through 29 years as a federal penitentiary, holding some of the nation's most desperate and uncontrollable criminals, *The Rock* claimed the lives of only three guards and ten convicts in escape attempts.

Some of the credit for this low casulty rate must go to the extensive training given those first guards, and to Warden Johnston's insistence on the highest guard-to-convict ratio in American penal history. Alcatraz had one guard to every three prisoners. The average in other American prisons was one guard to seven prisoners.

The warden had other techniques which he brought into play as the initial complement of gangsters learned respect for *The Rock*. These techniques were not those of his San Quentin days. Yet in the only way feasible on Alcatraz, they seemed to partake of that same personal understanding and integrity which he had shown as a young reform warden.

Having denied himself the inducement-tools of a prisoner rehabilitation program, Warden Johnston found ways of making life on Alcatraz endurable. To just endure one's life is not much. But to make a prisoner's life endurable on *The Rock* was a feat. Johnston's colleagues will always remember him for accomplishing that feat.

Perhaps the most effective tool Johnston used to divert his charges from acts of final despair was himself—the man. Prisoners call wardens their "chief inmates" and as *The Rock's* Chief Inmate Johnston is credited with being one of the least hated wardens in American penology.

He never sought to win the inmates' approval, but his quiet tone of voice (he is said never to have shouted), his unbroken word, his record of never basing punishment on stoolie information, his way of hearing a prisoner out, of not interrupting the petitioner, and of *explaining* his refusals, all gave the men a feeling that their chief inmate was fair—and consistent—consistently fair and consistently hard, but fair. Such a feeling might well have made for many of them that hairline of difference between utter despair and the ability to keep going.

He had other measures in his warden's repertoire. He informed the Bureau of Prisons that his inmates would have the best meals served in any prison of the country, and the bureau acquiesced. Alcatraz inmates often gained weight during their terms, for while bureau regulation prescribed a diet of 2100 calories daily *The Rock's* inmates consumed between 3100 and 3600 calories a day.

Colors, the Warden felt, were important in an inmate's environment. To relieve the often fog-shrouded grimness of *The Rock* he painted the cells, the walls, corridors even workshop doors and interiors in pastel greens, mauves, pinks. Blue was an accent color. Some of this unconventional decor is still there.

The men were issued three packs of cigarettes per week, and tobacco dispensers were placed where they could roll their own if they ran short of cigarettes. Tobacco had no currency value in the prisoners' economy at Alcatraz.

But most of all it was Johnston's understanding of the things that made a man a criminal, and the things a criminal felt, that give his warden's hand the sure touch. Once, when asked to list the common factors which landed his charges on *The Rock*, he wrote:

"…their antecedent histories, childhood influences, associations of youth, deprivations, excesses, gang connections, nomadic wanderings, neglect of health, law-breaking and all the *accrued results* of irregular and precarious living…."

Johnston did not regard the detection of insanity in a prisoner as a major problem. Usually its presence became obvious after a few hours of observation. More troublesome and "far more numerous than the insane," he wrote, "are the difficult-to-define psychopaths and psychoneurotics."

He knew what went on in a prisoner's mind and emotions. The so-called well prisoner, the man who seemed to be "making it okay" he believed suffered from an awareness of the stigma his crime had brought to his family, from "remorse, loss of self respect, inability to adjust or accept the situation, to take the blame for his predicament, or to take interest in his surroundings."

Johnston's insight, professional as it was, sprang from the well-springs of his own spirit. He was capable of bringing liberality to reactionary situations, as witnessed in his often expressed belief that every inmate bore daily distress because he could not cope with domestic and financial difficulties from behind bars— "including persons and situations he may have neglected while free."

The warden who built and ran *The Rock* knew that every inmate lived with despondency, that total despair was a constant threat, that the future appeared dark "because of an extreme sentence, loss of credits, sometimes knowing that at the end of a long term he will be re-arrested and taken to another prison."

And of course he was acutely aware of that prison horror which for centuries has lurked behind the public euphemism "intolerable prison conditions"—the practice of homosexuality by the "Daddies" and the "Queens," the bullies and the bullied, the latter sometimes willingly, sometimes under threat of death or fearsome reprisal from "Daddy's friends." Warden Johnston believed that "sexual starvation and inner conflicts over homosexual urges, or as a result of homosexual assault" were major despair factors in prison life.

Fear, just plain fear, is another dread companion of prison existence, he said— the inmate's fear for his health, fear of "pain, heat, cold, rain, dampness, fog, fatigue, anything and everything, real and imaginary."

He understood well the traumatic effect of *The Rock* and its rules upon the prisoner's psyche. He knew that every man's spirit hurt daily from "restraint of movement, monotony, routine, and sameness of associates, clothing, food, sentence, outlook—all deepening an ingrown attitude from constant feeding upon his small world."

Having produced this ruthless and overpowering discipline, Johnston then set about making it as endurable as he could.

Work, "just plain honest-to-goodness work," he said, is the strongest agent of reform. But work on the island wasn't the incentive that it is in more conventional prisons. *The Rock* had no reform program. Its sole purpose was to contain and punish. Men serving "Life" and 30- to 99-year sentences thought little of the credits they might earn by turning to prison jobs with a genuine will.

But willing or not, under Johnston they did work. Using his prestige and influence wherever it would open doors, the warden in due time put *The Rock* in business.

The inmates found themselves doing laundry for the Army and Navy facilities in the Bay Area; they made furniture, repaired shoes, manufactured brushes, opened a dry-cleaning plant, made clothing, manufactured fiber mats and did much of *The Rock's* routine maintenance. "The work," Johnston said, would "lessen mental strains...relax their tightly wound emotional threads."

And so it seemed because in its 29 years as the nation's sternest penitentiary *The Rock* counted a lower suicide and self-mutilation rate among inmates than did many conventional prisons.

No official announcement ever was made but at some point during those first four years the Warden and the Bureau must have had *The Rock's* discipline program under review—because it began to change. The over-all discipline never let up, but certain privileges began to arrive.

By 1937 the "Rule of Silence" had been eliminated. In 1945 the men could see one movie a month in an improvised prison theater. A library had been organized, with fiction, reference and periodical sections. Books could even by taken to cells and there was a prison band.

As early as 1940 the mail restrictions were relaxed. Inmates could correspond with two relatives instead of just one. When Warden Johnston retired in 1948 inmates in good standing could pursue approved projects and hobbies in their cells. More, they could keep the equipment for those pursuits in their cubicles, including their own books, drawing materials, writing paper and learning aids. They could relieve the barren walls of their five-by-eight "rooms" with pictures, religious objects and other approved decorations.

Johnston was succeeded by Wardens Edwin B. Swope, 1948-55, Paul J. Madigan, 1955-61 and Olin G. Blackwell. Blackwell took over from Madigan and closed *The Rock* on orders of Attorney General Robert F. Kennedy.

The introduction of minimum privileges continued under Johnston's successors. Madigan, a former Chief of Guards at Alcatraz, installed cell radios and prisoners could listen to sounds from the outside world during the long evening hours between lockup and lights-out. Madigan also did away with the bread-and-water diet in the "hole" cells. Prisoners doing time in solitary were given a modified version of the regular menu.

Though living conditions and atmosphere may have relaxed, the penalties for infraction of rules did not. Loss of privilege, loss of good-time credits, and sometimes even an additional sentence were bosom companions of "solitary." They waited like predestined fate for the unwary prisoner caught breaking *The Rock's* rules.

By and large these punishments served their purpose, to keep the inmate community under control. But some men for whatever reason are driven by emotional need to confront death rather than accept their plight. Every prison has its cadre of menace, men who never stop planning, watching, waiting for that moment when they will place their own and others' lives on destiny's line.

Considering its long-term population, Alcatraz had astonishingly few escape attempts and an even better average of successful tries. During its life as a federal penitentiary it hosted only fourteen actual attempts. Only 39 men took the desperate chance. Of these 26 were caught, seven were killed, one drowned and five were never seen again. Whether the five made it or drowned in the bay still is debatable.

Lifers and long-termers are the men most likely to make the all-or-nothing try, and the most likely to kill while trying. As nearly as records reveal, only ten or eleven of the 39 were men with sentences less than 25 years. At least 17 of the 39 were doing longer stretches and eleven were lifers.

"The Battle of Alcatraz" (May 2, 3 and 4, 1946) was between a die-hard trio composed of two lifers and a long-term bank robber and *The Rock's* guards. It was led by a remarkable prisoner, Joseph "Dutch" Cretzer. Cretzer, a lifer, and his companions died in the attempt. So also did two prison officers.

Cretzer was one of America's "public enemies" in the latter '30s. Starting in the early '20s he had graduated to the public enemy list through a series of bloodless gang exploits rivaling those of the bloodier Alvin Karpis and his mob.

From the moment he landed on *The Rock* in the late '30s Cretzer was an emotional bomb. He captured and tied up four guards in the machineshop on May 21, 1944, in what turned out to be an aborted escape. Cretzer gave up when one of the captured guards, from his prone position on the floor, convinced him that no emery wheel would cut through steel bars. The aborted attempt drew no blood but Cretzer vowed that the next time he would have guns.

The next time came two years later to the month. Nobody will ever know how long it took Cretzer to put his second escape plan together, probably all of the two years intervening the 1944 and 1946 attempts. Professional post mortems of "The Battle" agree that Cretzer and his co-conspirators must have made exhaustive, microscopic studies of the prison's routine, exceptions to that routine, personnel, armament and physical plant. They probably would have succeeded except for that inevitable happenstance which so often wrecks the best laid plans.

May 2, 1946, was a Thursday. Cretzer's
plan was ready for execution. With him in
the breakout were perhaps a dozen men
who would fade away as the battle wore
on, plus a hard core cadre of four, two
of whom would stick to him to the end and
two of whom would not but would be
executed later for their roles.

The four were Bernard Coy, long-termer;
Marion Thompson, lifer; Sam Shockley,
lifer; and Marvin Hubbard, long-termer.
Coy, Cretzer and Hubbard would die.
Shockley and Thompson would be ex-
ecuted.

Coy and Hubbard commenced the action.
They were the clean-up crew that day
in the mess hall, separated from the
main cell house only by the big swinging
iron grill doors which were guarded by
Officer William A. Miller.

Lunch had been uneventful. Inmates
having work assignments had been
counted and marched to their jobs. Others
were locked in their tiered cells. The
immense interior of the house-within-a-
house was very quiet in the early afternoon.

When the unarmed Officer Miller stooped
to search Hubbard as the men were de-
parting the mess hall, Coy struck him from
behind. Together the two men quietly
beat Miller into unconsciousness, found
his keys, swung open the iron grill doors
and threw the guard into a nearby cell,
No. 402.

With Miller's keys they stealthily released
Cretzer, Sam Shockley, Marion Thompson
and one other convict who on that day was
not yet 21 years of age. It was the imme-
diate job of these first-released men to
take the gun gallery on the interior catwalk
above them. So far they had not been
seen or heard by the guard. The uncon-
scious Miller had made no sound after
the first blow.

The gun gallery was screened by wire
mesh. From behind it the armed guard
had a balcony view (thus the term "gun
gallery"), of the main cell block. The
gallery also continued along the main wall
into D block, or the "treatment unit" as
the cons termed it because it was used
for isolated prisoners and it contained the

dreaded solitary "hole" cells. When the guard was surveying D block he could not see or hear anything from the main cell blocks for a moment. A door and a wall separated the isolation cells from the rest of the prison.

Taking advantage of those precious moments, Cretzer's cadre hastily fashioned a makeshift "bar spreader" from pipes and plumbing fixtures they had liberated (using Miller's keys) from a locked utility corridor. Hubbard and Coy monkey-climbed the wire mesh from "Broadway's" floor up to the bars guarding the balcony. They spread them enough to let Coy slip through onto the gallery's floor.

Coy crouched, waiting behind the gallery door separating D block from the main house. When the guard came through on his way back from checking D block Coy slugged him into unconsciousness and tied him up. He flipped the guard's revolver down to the waiting Cretzer and arming himself with the guard's rifle and ammunition belt rejoined Cretzer on "Broadway."

Next Cretzer and Coy went to the thick steel door which separated D block from the main house on the ground floor. They knocked. When the guard opened the slit to see who it was Cretzer thrust the revolver muzzle through and had the guard in his sights. The guard opened the door and was slugged into unconsciousness.

When the groundfloor door connecting D block with the rest of the main cellhouse opened Cretzer and his cadre "owned" the main cell house. Thus news of the growing breakout had not gone beyond the interior of the cell house.

The cell community was now electrified. Some inmates had aided Cretzer and his men by keeping up a series of ordinary but consistent noises from their cells, to cover the muffled blows, grunts, threats and movement of bodies below. Those who could see the action were passing whispered reports to those who could not. Some prisoners went to the rear of their cells so as not to know what was transpiring. If they didn't know, they couldn't testify later.

Cretzer now had an assortment of guards' keys. He opened the cell doors of the main block, freeing the prisoners who began to fill "Broadway." But he couldn't open one whole section of cells in the isolation unit, D block. The locks were electrically controlled from a switch outside the main cell house. He did, however, free about thirty of the men in the "treatment unit."

Up to this moment, Cretzer's plan had rolled along like a juggernaut. But as the exultant leader tried to find the right key for the door leading to the recreation yard he was surrounded by a nervously sweating, hoarsely whispering, pushing, shoving mob of cons. His hands shook as he tried key after key. Finally it was clear that Cretzer's plan had hit a snag. The key wasn't there.

It wasn't there because Officer Miller, its custodian, had hidden it. To this day no unofficial person knows how or where Miller concealed that vital key.

The enraged Cretzer rushed back to Cell 402. Savagely he beat the now conscious Miller. Miller steadfastly refused to reveal the key's whereabouts. Finally he lost consciousness again under Cretzer's fierce blows.

Cretzer's plan was stalled. The men were out of their cells but they couldn't go anywhere. They were prisoners inside the main cell house. The leaders, Cretzer, Coy and Hubbard, must have known what the end would be then. There was only one sentence waiting for them now.

The others, the small fry who had made noises in their cells and covered the sounds of escape, the opportunists who had crowded up to the recreation yard door and even two of the original cadre, faded away. Only Cretzer, Coy and Hubbard carried on the fight. They made their stand from inside the main cell house.

It is estimated that the break was in progress approximately 50 minutes when, at 2:30 P.M., an officer overseeing prisoners at work in the basement suspected something wrong when a group of prissoners he told to return to their cells came back down the stairs. He went to the top of the stairs and called for Miller. When there was no answer he descended the stairs and phoned the armory. The armory called the warden.

Meanwhile inside the cell house a total of five officers who had been ambushed as they entered the cell house on routine errands, were locked into cells 402 and 403.

Warden Johnston ordered a general alarm. Four officers, unaware that the prisoners had guns, rushed into the main cell house and were captured by Cretzer and Coy at gunpoint. They were locked into cells 402 and 403 with their colleagues including the now dying Miller. In all, Cretzer had ten hostages.

Off-duty officers came running from the island quarters to the armory where Johnston had set up his command post. They drew weapons and ammunition. Johnston deployed them to strategic areas. Word of the break was flashed to Washington, to federal agencies concerned, the Coast Guard, the San Francisco Police Department, and to military units in the bay area.

The hopeless fight went on for 40 more hours. Coast Guard cutters circled the island. A small contingent of marines landed. Spotter planes patrolled overhead. Reinforcements, material and human, were flown into San Francisco from Englewood, McNeil Island and Leavenworth. The nation's public media headlined "The Battle of Alcatraz" for three days, and spent months more analyzing it.

Tower officers came under prisoner fire. One tower guard was shot in both legs. Six of the imprisoned officers were wounded when Cretzer, hearing the general alarm and sensing the end. hysterically fired his revolver point blank into the guards crowded into cells 402 and 403.

When it became clear to Johnston that the missing officers all had to be somewhere in the main cell house, he decided to retake the gun gallery. If his men could command that position the armed prisoners below could be driven by gunfire into positions behind blocks C and B. Then the cell house could be searched for the missing officers.

The gallery was retaken by a direct charge, under fire from Cretzer and Coy. Officer Harold P. Stites was fatally wounded in the charge. The gun gallery officer was found gagged and bound but unhurt. He was able to tell his rescuers how many guns the escapers had and where the ambushed guards had been placed.

Dusk had come and the cell house was dark. Cretzer, Coy and Hubbard could dodge in and out of cells as the guards sought to drive them to cover behind C and B blocks. At times the guards were under fire from the tops of the cell blocks.

At ten o'clock that first night Alcatraz officers, despite shots from atop the blocks, managed to take out the six wounded officers, the dying Miller and three other guards from cells 402 and 403.

When Cretzer and his partners saw armed guards down on the main floor they became fearful of crossfire from the gallery above and took refuge in a long, narrow utility corridor which ran lengthwise between C and B blocks.

Then the officers took to the cell tops, punched holes in the roof of the utility corridor and dropped demolition grenades into it, driving the three men into a still smaller pipe tunnel.

The usually spic and span main cell house was a shambles. "Broadway's" usual sheen was obscured with the litter of battle, waste and other objects thrown by nonparticipating prisoners from their cells. The air was a smog of steam, tear gas and gunsmoke.

Sometime during that late afternoon, after the escapers had been driven into their hole, the guards marched all the other prisoners into the recreation yard where they spent the night under guard by eight marines. Only the men still locked in their cells in the "treatment unit" remained under the cell house roof.

The fight went on through Thursday night into Friday morning. The nonparticipants who had spent the night in the yard were herded back into their cells during a lull in the firing. The guards felt that Cretzer, Coy and Hubbard now must be holed up either in the utilities corridor or in a small connecting pipe tunnel. Also, they could be hiding in D block. Both sides had held their fire for several hours. Then at 5 P.M. shots came from inside the utilities corridor of C block, informing the guards that the escapers definitely were not in D block.

Watches were set up at both ends of the utility corridor and the rest of the prison secured for the night.

Saturday at cool gray 6 A.M. the guards commenced a cautious search of the C block utilities corridor, first firing shotgun and rifle into the dark passageway. There was no answering fire. Two guards with flashlights went in. They found Cretzer dead, his revolver beside the body. Coy, also dead, still cradled the rifle, and Hubbard whose body was still warm, appeared to have just expired. From a count of the depleted ammunition carriers it appeared that the trio had fired 25 rifle shots and 21 rounds from the revolver. *The Rock's* biggest break was over. Later Thompson and Shockley were executed for their share in the attempt.

Though *The Rock's* "biggest battle" proved the holding power, albeit at some cost, of Warden Johnston's creation, not all attempted escapes ended so conclusively. Five men did succeed in disappearing from the island prison. Whether they lived or died still makes interesting argument among old prison hands. Alcatraz and Prison Bureau officials maintain that the five most likely drowned in the bay's swift tides and chill temperatures.

But San Francisco Bay's tides are not uniformly all that tough. There are days in the year when the tide is slower, softer and not so vicious with its speed. Then too, serious speculation must take into account the adrenalin-derived extra strength of the escaper as he makes that last desperate bid.

And there were the swimming aids which were found after several attempted escapes, small rafts, crude Mae Wests and water wings made from rubber gloves, the sleeves of plastic raincoats, and other ingenious floatables. Some, or even all, of the five *might* have made it.

After all, Anastasia "Babe" Scott, a San Francisco high-school swimmer, had swum from the island to the Dolphin Club dock at the foot of Hyde Street in 47 minutes in 1933. Several Dolphin Club members had swum it to the 300 yards warning area and back.

There were two escapes into oblivion if not freedom, the first in 1937 and the second in 1962. The first, that of Theodore Cole and Ralph Roe, bank robbers serving long terms, was relatively simple, quick— and final.

Cole and Roe established excellent behavior records and were given jobs in the mat factory. Fog was the key element in their escape plan. December 16, 1937, brought one of the bay area's heaviest fogs and the pair, that morning, decided to make their run.

They waited until after lunch. Back at the mat factory they busied themselves at work until the guard had made his first prisoner count. Then one of them ran from the mat factory to the machine shop, grabbed a large wrench and a pipe, and made it back to the mat shop without being seen.

Willing collaborators elevated the shop noise level as the pair went to work on a shop window overlooking the catwalk below. Outside the fog swirled thickly and the bay's foghorns moaned their mournful slow chant.

The steel sashing gave way. The escapers wriggled through and dropped to the catwalk 20 feet below. The guard in the tower above was lost in the heavy gray mist and could see nothing.

Feeling their way along the enclosing wire mesh of the catwalk, Cole and Roe came to the gate, forced its padlock, passed through and leaped again, this time a blind jump onto a collection of old rubber tires which luckily, or perhaps more probably by design, happened to be there. If they had missed the tires their bodies would have struck jagged rock before bouncing into the bay.

The trail ended there. The wrench and pipe are said to have been found on those rocks. Cole and Roe were never traced.

The second escape-without-a-trace was more elaborate and had a touch of humor. By 1962 *The Rock* was 28 years old as a civilian penitentiary. Twenty-eight years of continuous escape talk among the cons, remembered and passed on to each newcomer by word of mouth, had built a substantial body of escape lore. Much of it was myth and infeasible, but not all of it. And there was one man of exceptional intelligence who made it his business to listen, sift through the myth and the impractical and learn. He was Frank Lee Morris, a 35-year-old bank robber doing a long stretch.

Morris was a short and slight man, so it was natural that he would look for size and brawn in his cohorts. He chose two brothers, young, big and strong. They were Clarence and John Anglin, also bank robbers.

Morris' plan took account of every scrap of con talk available in the prison community. To his gleanings of feasible escape routes, he added another element from his own observations. *The Rock* was getting old. Concrete could be seen drying and crumbling away from iron supports, rust stained the pipes outside the building, the maintenance work had increased substantially in 1960 and 1961. *The Rock's* own natural aging process gave Morris the touchstone for the trio's successful disappearance.

Months before the escape the trio had captured key jobs from which they extracted materials for one of the most amazing escape kits ever seen in penal history.

From Morris' jobs in the machine and furniture shops came the hardware, the chisels and mallets with which each of the trio chipped away the weakened concrete around his cell air vent. From the younger Anglin brother's job in the clothes factory came the plastic raincoat sleeves which became crude Mae West swimming vests. The other Anglin was a barber. He supplied the hair for the plastic, painted heads which peeped out from the trio's blankets all through the escape night, June 12, 1962, lulling the guards during the hourly checks and giving the trio a nine-hour lead on their pursuers.

It took months to enlarge the air vent openings enough to permit passage of a human body. The work had to be done between hourly guard counts. Friendly and timely music practice by members of the Alcatraz band covered the noise of tapping hammers. During the day the holes were covered by excellently executed paintings of the air vent, done on cardboard. Dust and dirt were carried out in pockets and scattered as the escapers went about their work on the island.

Morris had determined the route to be through the air vent holes into the utility corridor, then up the pipe-maze which filled the narrow alley to the top of the cell block, directly under the mouth of the huge air vent which circulated air through the entire main cell house. From there they would exit through the big vent and cross roof tops, descend walls and make their way to the bay waters.

One of the Anglin brothers convinced the prison administration that a blanket should be hung up close to the cell house ceiling to keep paint flakings from drifting down into the tiers.

This gave him an excuse for ascending to the top of the cell block at least once a week for a few moments, obstensibly to remove the accumulated flakings from the blanket. The blanket screened him as over a period of several weeks he loosened the bolts holding the heavy screening which covered the vent's mouth.

All was in readiness, Monday, June 11, 1962. The trio moved through the day's routine, seemingly quiet and resigned to the monotony of another routine day. But their pulses must have accelerated because they had chosen that night to make their run for it.

A few minutes after lights out and the final bed check, three forms emerged in the dark pipe-maze corridor between cell blocks. They ascended the pipes to the cell block roof, silently removed the loosened screen from the big vent and squirmed up through its shaft to the outside roof.

On the roof they successfully dodged the sweeping searchlights and went down one of the walls, probably the north wall—or could they have descended into the recreation yard, then scaled the big yard's south wall and so proceeded to the cove beneath the big incinerator?

Nobody really knows. They went. They were never seen again.

Only one "clue" was found, and it might have been a deliberate plant to make authorities believe they had drowned. At week's end searchers came across a plastic wallet washed up on the Marin shore north of San Francisco. In it were papers belonging to one of the Anglin brothers.

Later, reconstructing that night's conditions, authorities found that the tides had been mild. The chase spread to every part of the United States and covered all national ports. To no avail. Officials said the trio must have drowned.

But who is to say that Morris, with his extraordinary patience, attention to detail, and intellect, did not have outside connections to assist the trio in their onward flight?

Only one more, unsuccessful, escape attempt occurred before Alcatraz closed down. On December 16, 1962, Paul Scott and Darl Parker, serving long terms for bank robbery, made it into the bay moments before their absence was noted and the alarm given. Scott, a strong swimmer, was picked up an hour later, exhausted, lying in the rocks below Fort Point on the San Francisco side of the Golden Gate. Parker got as far as "Little Alcatraz" where he clung, numbed and almost in shock, until a prison boat brought him back to Big Alcatraz.

During its nearly 29 years of service as the world's tightest penitentiary, Alcatraz was not without some victories. The island hosted more than 1500 prisoners. Some 800 of them "earned" their way to other less grim prisons. More than 200 were conditionally released and about 75 served their full terms and went back to society, their debts paid.

Over the years the nature of its convict population changed, from big-time mobsters out of the Prohibition era to a collection of lesser criminals. The need for the unique citadel was over by 1962 when the late Attorney General Robert F. Kennedy ordered its close-down.

The Rock was to have only one more headline to flash. In 1969 it was "captured" by a small band of American Indians who occupied the empty buildings for several months, claiming the island as Indian territory under the clauses of an old treaty.

The Nation was aware of their presence on the island. Headlines blared in all media. San Franciscans on clear nights could see their bonfires. And, sometimes when the wind was right, the faint sounds of their chantings would reach the ears of tourists thronging Fisherman's Wharf.

In the specific sense their occupation of *The Rock* achieved little. Even their ancestors of de Ayala's time were reputed to have considered the barren waterless island a "bad place," perhaps haunted. The logistics of water, food, sanitation and warmth were against the new settlers. The federal government, aware of a growing-public concern for the plight of our American Indian citizens, took no precipitate action, but simply waited them out. The small band was removed peaceably in 1971 and *The Rock* again had only the company of wind. fog, the tides, seagulls, cormorants and a few remaining pelicans.

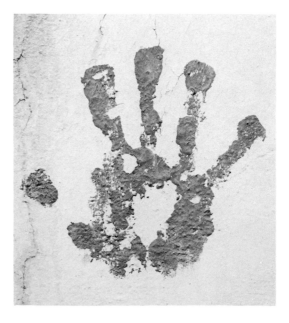

But in a broader sense the American Indian occupation cast *The Rock* in a new role; after all, nobody before had volunteered to live there. The boldness and resolve of the small group won the sympathy, if not the approval, of many Americans who hold the view that the American Indian citizen today needs, and should have, more help from a responsive and understanding nation. Perhaps in this short postscript event *The Rock's* long record of negative service may yet find a turning.